Caramels

Dedication

To my wonderful children, Basile and Eloise.
—Elisabeth Antoine

To my wonderful husband, Rich, and my two
darling daughters, Olivia and Isabelle.
—Elizabeth Cunningham Herring

Acknowledgments

We would like to thank our families and friends for their support and patience with us as we experimented with different recipes.

We would especially like to thank Julia Erickson and Julie Pauly and The Able Baker crew for all their help and support.

We would also like to thank our agent, Coleen O'Shea, and our publisher, Robin Haywood.

Published by Sellers Publishing, Inc.
Text and photography copyright © 2012 Elisabeth Antoine & Elizabeth Cunningham Herring
All rights reserved.

Sellers Publishing, Inc.
161 John Roberts Road, South Portland, Maine 04106
Visit our Web site: www.sellerspublishing.com
E-mail: rsp@rsvp.com

ISBN 13: 978-1-4162-0695-8
e-ISBN: 978-1-4162-0863-1
Library of Congress Control Number: 2012931588

10 9 8 7 6 5 4 3 2 1

Printed and bound in China.

Caramels

Gooey, Chewy Delights

Text and Photography by
ELISABETH ANTOINE and ELIZABETH CUNNINGHAM HERRING

SELLERS
PUBLISHING

Contents

Coffee Caramels

Toffee, Brittle, Sauces, and Bars

Introduction

S oft, chewy, buttery, sweet, there's just nothing like caramel. It stirs something inside. So simple and yet so delicious.

This sweet candy has a long and rich history. Seventeenth century American colonists boiled water and sugar together in deep kettles — caramelizing the sugar in the process — to create hard candies. They were inexpensive and easy to make and had a long shelf life.

It wasn't until the middle of the 19th century, however, that the soft creamy caramels we're so familiar with came into existence. It was discovered that by adding cream to the sugary mix you could transform it into a heavenly chewy confection. Milton Hershey of the eponymous company was the first to come up with the idea of covering caramel with chocolate. And an amazing new flavor combination was born.

In fact, caramel is a chameleon that can easily inhabit a host of different flavors. Nuts and fruits can add a wonderful texture, and liqueur and spices can create entirely new taste sensations.

Though caramels are widely available and not very costly, most store-bought varieties do not do justice to this succulent confection. Once you have tasted a homemade caramel, you will be smitten for life.

Fortunately caramels are surprisingly easy to make as long as you have the right equipment. Those just starting out will definitely need a candy thermometer. Once you have one that has been calibrated properly, you can easily make any recipe in this book. We give you a detailed step-by-step guide to making caramels as well as instructions on how to dip and decorate them so they look as if they were made by a professional. The how-to part is followed by four sections: the first focuses on vanilla caramel variations, the second on chocolate, the third on coffee, and the last features recipes for caramel-based desserts such as toffee, brittle, sauces, and bars.

Since caramels are beloved by just about everyone, they make wonderful gifts. The book concludes with a chapter on how to creatively package caramels.

So grab this book and your candy thermometer and go to town experimenting with different flavor combinations. You will be rewarded with a warm, fragrant kitchen and happy neighbors and friends.

How to Make Caramels

Many people approach caramel making with some trepidation. Perhaps it's the candy thermometer that makes them nervous. Have no fear. Caramels are not as difficult to make as one might think. The recipes in this book are all pretty foolproof. If you follow the step-by-step instructions on the following pages carefully, you will be rewarded with a delicious pan of soft, but firm and chewy, caramels. Make sure to calibrate your candy thermometer before you start (see page 17).

For the basic caramel recipe, you will need the following tools: 5-quart saucepan with tall sides, 9 X 9-inch pan, parchment paper, wooden spoon, mug of warm water, pastry brush, calibrated candy thermometer, measuring spoons, measuring cups, and a sharp knife.

1.

Place the pastry brush in the mug of warm water. You can also place the thermometer there to keep it handy.

2.

Prepare your pan by lightly oiling it.

3.

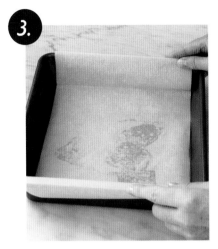

Place in the pan a piece of parchment paper cut to the width of the pan but a little longer on the sides as shown.

4.

Place all your ingredients in the saucepan except the flavorings. The basic Classic Vanilla Caramel recipe includes: sugar, light brown sugar, corn syrup, honey, evaporated milk, heavy cream, unsalted butter, and salt. Make sure the butter is cut into small pieces so it melts easily.

Put the saucepan on the stove over medium heat and gently stir the ingredients with a wooden spoon until the sugar is dissolved, the butter is melted, and the mixture is smooth. Stop stirring and do not stir again until step 9.

Increase the heat to medium high and allow the mixture to come to a boil, letting it bubble up.

7. Brush the sides of the saucepan above the bubbling caramel regularly with the pastry brush dipped in warm water. This will keep the caramel from crystallizing.

8. Regularly check the temperature of the caramel with the thermometer. Make sure the thermometer doesn't touch the bottom of the saucepan. Some thermometers come with a clip that allows you to attach them to the saucepan. This may be more convenient than constantly dipping your thermometer in the caramel, but we find that you will get a more accurate reading from the middle of the saucepan.

9. When the temperature reaches 250°F (121°C) remove the pot from the heat and add the vanilla, mixing well with the wooden spoon. Make sure the vanilla is thoroughly mixed in.

10. Pour the caramel into the prepared pan.

11.

Let the caramel cool in the pan for a few hours at room temperature. If you want to speed up the process, you can put the pan in the refrigerator after it has cooled at room temperature for one hour. (You should bring the caramel back to room temperature before cutting it.)

12.

When the caramel is set, invert the pan onto another piece of parchment paper and peel off the original parchment.

Cut the caramel into squares (or any shape you like) with a sharp knife.

Store cut caramels between parchment paper in a resealable storage container in the refrigerator so they keep their shape. When stored properly, the caramels will keep for a month.

There are several ways to serve caramels. The easiest method is to wrap small squares in candy papers.

How to Calibrate Your Candy Thermometer

One reason many people think caramel making is difficult is that if the temperature of the caramel is just a few degrees off, the caramel will not turn out. Too high a temperature and it will be too hard, too low a temperature and it will be too soft. It is an exact science. So it is important to check the accuracy of your candy thermometer. You only have to do this once, but it's crucial that you don't skip this step.

Fill a medium saucepan with water. Clip your candy thermometer to the side of the saucepan, making sure that it is submerged by at least 2 inches, but that it is not touching the bottom or sides of the saucepan. Bring the water to a boil and let it boil for 10 minutes. Check the temperature on your candy thermometer. It should read 212°F (100°C). (Note: This is the temperature at which water boils at sea level; this reading may be different depending upon where you live, so make sure you find out at what temperature water boils in your area before you start.) If your thermometer boils water at a few degrees over, say, 215°F, then you need to add 3 degrees when you use it. Of course, if your thermometer boils water at 210°F, you should subtract 2 degrees when you use it. You may want to use an indelible marker to write "add 3" or "subtract 2" on your thermometer so you always remember to make the adjustment. Now your candy thermometer is calibrated and you're ready to begin!

English Toffee, page 102

Caramel Making Safety Tips

When you make caramel you are heating sugar to a very high temperature. You definitely want to be cautious. Here are a few tips to keep you safe in the kitchen:

- Make sure to use a sturdy saucepan. Note that the caramel is going to boil vigorously for about 20 minutes, so you want to make sure you have a large enough saucepan to accommodate the bubbling liquid.

- Never leave boiling caramel unattended.

- You may wish to wear oven mitts and even a long-sleeve shirt to avoid getting burned as you check the temperature.

- Be careful when adding ingredients, as caramel can splatter.

Coating and Dipping Your Caramels

Caramels are a versatile candy. The chewy morsels are delicious on their own, of course, but their flavor can be enhanced by either coating them with a favorite topping or dipping them in chocolate.

Though most of the caramel recipes in this book feature either plain caramels or caramels dipped in chocolate, the recipe for Apricot Almond Vanilla Caramels (page 34) calls for rolling a piece of caramel into a ball as you would a truffle and coating it with chopped almonds.

You can coat other caramels using the same method. Just make sure that the caramel is allowed to soften at room temperature for a half hour or so before you coat it in this manner (to ensure that the coating will stick).

Dipping caramels in chocolate requires a bit more time, but the results are well worth it. Glossy and smooth, caramels dipped in chocolate are also delicious, as chocolate is always a wonderful addition to caramel. Dipping also allows you to top the chocolate covering with a nut or other small decoration to offer a clue to its interior flavor.

To start, you will need to temper your chocolate (see page 28) or use chocolate coating (see page 29).

1.

Get your equipment ready. Shown here are a medium heat-proof bowl, dipping tools, parchment paper, cutting board, sharp knife, and a serving plate for finished caramels.

2.

Place your tempered chocolate or melted chocolate coating in the bowl. Place a caramel on the dipping fork.

3.

Dip the caramel in the chocolate, making sure to cover it completely. (Tip: You may want to place the bowl on a heating pad set on low to sustain the temperature while you are dipping your caramels.)

4.

Gently scrape the excess chocolate from the bottom of the caramel on the edge of the bowl.

5.

Carefully place the caramel on parchment paper to dry.

6.

If you want to add a decoration, place it on the caramel before the coating dries.

7.

Carefully cut off any excess chocolate that may have formed on the bottom of the caramel when it was drying.

8.

If you would like to add a drizzle, place some melted chocolate in a resealable plastic bag.

9.

Snip off a tiny corner of the bag as shown.

10.

Carefully drizzle the chocolate over the caramels in any pattern you choose. Make sure the coating is dry before you drizzle on it.

11.

And you have a tray of lovely caramels.

How to Temper Chocolate

In order to achieve a smooth glossy finish, you will need to temper your chocolate before you dip the caramel in it. The easiest way to do this is to seed the chocolate.

Make sure to use quality chocolate with a high cocoa butter content, often labeled couverture chocolate. Chop the chocolate finely and place about half of it in a bain marie (or a heatproof bowl over a saucepan of simmering water). Stir every so often until the chocolate is fully melted. Check the temperature. For dark chocolate, it should be 115°F (46°C); for milk and white chocolate, it should read 110°F (43°C). Remove the bowl from the saucepan and place it on a dishtowel.

Now it is time to seed. Start adding the rest of the chocolate a little at a time, stirring it vigorously. When the additional chocolate has been added, check the temperature again. For dark, it should be 90°F (32°C) and for milk and white, it should be 88°F (31°C). The chocolate should have a shiny appearance.

You can test the chocolate by dipping a metal spoon in it and then placing the spoon in the refrigerator for a few minutes. If it looks glossy and firm when you take it out, it is good to go. If it's streaky or spotty, something went wrong in the process and you'll have to start over.

Tip: You may want to place the bowl on a heating pad set on low to sustain the temperature while you are dipping your caramels.

Dipping Option: Use Chocolate Coating

With patience, anyone can temper chocolate. However, tempering can be a bit challenging due to the fickle nature of chocolate. If you feel daunted by the prospect, fear not. There is an easier way, though you may have to sacrifice a little flavor.

Chocolate coating is widely available in supermarkets and craft stores and on the Internet. It's easy to use and, more importantly, absolutely foolproof. Chocolate coating usually comes with instructions, but most brands call for you to microwave the chocolate in a bowl for 30-second intervals at 30 percent power until it is melted and smooth. You'll find that the caramels dipped in chocolate coating dry much faster than those dipped in the tempered chocolate. They will also look perfect. However, the taste will not be as rich and chocolaty.

Vanilla Caramels

Classic Vanilla Caramels

If you have never had the pleasure of eating a homemade caramel, this basic recipe is a great introduction. And it's remarkably easy. The warm vanilla flavor accented with a subtle hint of honey will transport you to your happy place.

Makes about 72 caramels.

YOU WILL NEED

5-quart saucepan with tall sides
Pastry brush and a small mug of
  warm water
Wooden spoon
Calibrated candy thermometer

9 X 9-inch pan, oiled and lined
  with parchment paper
Sharp knife
Resealable container for storage

INGREDIENTS

2 cups sugar
1 cup light brown sugar, firmly
  packed
1/2 cup light corn syrup
1/2 cup honey
1 cup evaporated milk

2 cups heavy cream
1/2 cup unsalted butter, cut into
  pieces
Pinch of salt
2 teaspoons vanilla extract

Instructions:

In the saucepan, mix together the sugars, corn syrup, honey, evaporated milk, heavy cream, butter, and salt. Place the saucepan on the stove over medium heat and stir with the wooden spoon until all the sugar is dissolved, the butter is melted, and the mixture is smooth. Increase the heat to medium high and let the mixture boil without stirring. Brush the sides of the saucepan regularly with the pastry brush dipped in warm water to keep the caramel from crystallizing.

Check the temperature regularly with your candy thermometer until it reaches 250°F (121°C). (Be patient as it will take at least 20 minutes or so.) Then remove the saucepan from the heat and add the vanilla, stirring thoroughly to blend. Pour the caramel into the prepared pan and let it cool for a few hours. When set, invert the caramel onto a new piece of parchment paper and cut it into squares with the sharp knife.

Once cut, caramels should be stored in the resealable container in the refrigerator in order for them to keep their shape. Stored properly, caramels will keep for a month.

Apricot Almond Vanilla Caramels

These are a little different from the other caramels. Instead of cutting them into squares, we've made them into balls and rolled them in chopped almonds. They really stand out from the rest of the caramel crowd, and, in the gold foil liners, they make an elegant presentation.

Makes about 72 caramel balls.

YOU WILL NEED

2 small bowls
5-quart saucepan with tall sides
Pastry brush and a small mug of
　warm water
Wooden spoon

Calibrated candy thermometer
9 X 9-inch pan, oiled and lined
　with parchment paper
Resealable container for storage

INGREDIENTS

2/3 cup finely chopped dried apricots
2 tablespoons dark rum
1 teaspoon vanilla extract
1 teaspoon almond extract
1 teaspoon cinnamon
2 cups sugar
1 cup light brown sugar,
　firmly packed
1/2 cup light corn syrup

1/2 cup honey
1 cup evaporated milk
2 cups heavy cream
1/2 cup unsalted butter,
　cut into pieces
Pinch of salt

1 cup finely chopped almonds

Instructions:

In one small bowl, mix together the dried apricots and rum. Set aside. In another small bowl, mix together the vanilla, almond extract, and cinnamon. Set aside.

In the saucepan, mix together the sugars, corn syrup, honey, evaporated milk, heavy cream, butter, and salt. Place the saucepan on the stove over medium heat and stir with the wooden spoon until all the sugar is dissolved, the butter is melted, and the mixture is smooth. Increase the heat to medium high and let the mixture boil without stirring. Brush the sides of the saucepan regularly with the pastry brush dipped in warm water to keep the caramel from crystallizing.

Check the temperature regularly with your candy thermometer until it reaches 250°F (121°C). (Be patient as it will take at least 20 minutes or so.) Then remove the saucepan from the heat and add the vanilla mixture, stirring carefully. Add the soaked apricots and mix thoroughly to blend. Pour the caramel into the prepared pan and let it cool for a few hours. When set, invert the caramel onto a new piece of parchment paper and cut it into walnut-sized pieces. Roll each piece in your hands to form a ball and then roll it in the chopped almonds.

The caramel balls should be stored in the resealable container in the refrigerator in order for them to keep their shape. Stored properly, caramels will keep for a month.

Citrus Vanilla Caramels

Cool citrus and warm vanilla may seem like an unlikely pair, but take one bite and you'll realize it's a match made in heaven. Hints of orange and lemon zest bring a scintillating yet subtle note to the vanilla caramel. We must say it's a very pleasant sensation!

Makes about 72 caramels.

YOU WILL NEED

Zest grater
2 small bowls
5-quart saucepan with tall sides
Pastry brush and a small mug of
    warm water
Wooden spoon

Calibrated candy thermometer
9 X 9-inch pan, oiled and lined
    with parchment paper
Small strainer
Sharp knife
Resealable container for storage

INGREDIENTS

2 teaspoons vanilla extract
Zest of 1 orange
Zest of 1 lemon
2 cups sugar
1 cup light brown sugar,
    firmly packed
1/2 cup light corn syrup

1/2 cup honey
1 cup evaporated milk
2 cups heavy cream
1/2 cup unsalted butter,
    cut into pieces
Pinch of salt

Instructions:

In the small bowl, mix together the vanilla with the orange and lemon zests. Set aside for 30 minutes and then strain into a second bowl, discarding solids.

In the saucepan, mix together the sugars, corn syrup, honey, evaporated milk, heavy cream, butter, and salt. Place the saucepan on the stove over medium heat and stir with the wooden spoon until all the sugar is dissolved, the butter is melted, and the mixture is smooth. Increase the heat to medium high and let the mixture boil without stirring. Brush the sides of the pan regularly with the pastry brush dipped in warm water to keep the caramel from crystallizing.

Check the temperature regularly with your candy thermometer until it reaches 250°F (121°C). (Be patient as it will take at least 20 minutes or so.) Then remove the saucepan from the heat and add the strained vanilla/citrus mix, stirring thoroughly to blend. Pour the caramel into the prepared pan and let it cool for a few hours. When set, invert the caramel on a new piece of parchment paper and cut into squares with the sharp knife.

Once cut, caramels should be stored in the resealable container in the refrigerator in order for them to keep their shape. Stored properly, caramels will keep for a month.

Pistachio Vanilla Caramels

The light buttery flavor of pistachios are a perfect fit for vanilla caramels. The nuts also imbue the caramel with a lovely green color and a crunchy texture.

Makes about 72 caramels.

YOU WILL NEED

5-quart saucepan with tall sides
Pastry brush and a small mug of
  warm water
Wooden spoon
Calibrated candy thermometer

9 X 9-inch pan, oiled and lined
  with parchment paper
Sharp knife
Resealable container for storage

INGREDIENTS

2 cups sugar
1 cup light brown sugar,
  firmly packed
$\frac{1}{2}$ cup light corn syrup
$\frac{1}{2}$ cup honey
1 cup evaporated milk
2 cups heavy cream

$\frac{1}{2}$ cup unsalted butter,
  cut into pieces
1 teaspoon salt
2 teaspoon vanilla extract
1 teaspoon almond extract
1 cup pistachios, shelled and
  chopped

Instructions:

In the saucepan, mix together the sugars, corn syrup, honey, evaporated milk, heavy cream, butter, and salt. Place the saucepan on the stove over medium heat and stir with the wooden spoon until all the sugar is dissolved, the butter is melted, and the mixture is smooth. Increase the heat to medium high and let the mixture boil without stirring. Brush the sides of the saucepan regularly with the pastry brush dipped in warm water to keep the caramel from crystallizing.

Check the temperature regularly with your candy thermometer until it reaches 250°F (121°C). (Be patient as it will take at least 20 minutes or so.) Then remove the saucepan from the heat and add the vanilla and almond extracts and the pistachios. Stir thoroughly to blend. Pour the caramel into the prepared pan and let it cool for a few hours. When set, invert the caramel onto a new piece of parchment paper and cut it into squares with the sharp knife.

Once cut, caramels should be stored in the resealable container in the refrigerator in order for them to keep their shape. Stored properly, caramels will keep for a month.

Cardamom Vanilla Caramels

The intense orange-herb aroma of cardamom is a natural partner for mild vanilla. Together they infuse caramel with a delicious exotic flavor.

Makes about 72 caramels.

YOU WILL NEED

Small bowl
5-quart saucepan with tall sides
Pastry brush and a small mug of
   warm water
Wooden spoon
Calibrated candy thermometer

9 X 9-inch pan, oiled and lined
   with parchment paper
Sharp knife
Bain marie
Fork or dipping tools
Resealable container for storage

INGREDIENTS

2 tablespoons vanilla extract
2 teaspoons ground cardamom
2 cups sugar
1 cup light brown sugar,
   firmly packed
1/2 cup light corn syrup
1/2 cup honey
1 cup evaporated milk

2 cups heavy cream
1/2 cup unsalted butter,
   cut into pieces

30 ounces milk chocolate, finely
   chopped and divided
Cardamom powder for decoration
   (optional)

Instructions:

In the small bowl, mix together the vanilla and cardamom. Set aside.

In the saucepan, mix together the sugars, corn syrup, honey, evaporated milk, heavy cream, and butter. Place the saucepan on the stove over medium heat and stir with the wooden spoon until all the sugar is dissolved, the butter is melted, and the mixture is smooth. Increase the heat to medium high and let the mixture boil without stirring. Brush the sides of the saucepan regularly with the pastry brush dipped in warm water to keep the caramel from crystallizing.

Check the temperature regularly with your candy thermometer until it reaches 250°F (121°C). (Be patient as it will take at least 20 minutes or so.) Then remove the saucepan from the heat and add the vanilla mixture, stirring thoroughly to blend. Pour the caramel into the prepared pan and let it cool for a few hours. When set, invert the caramel onto a new piece of parchment paper and cut it into squares with the sharp knife.

(recipe continues on next page)

Cardamom Vanilla Caramels (continued)

To make the chocolate coating, place 20 ounces of the chopped milk chocolate in the bain marie (bowl over a saucepan ¼ full of water). Heat the water over medium-low heat and gently stir the chocolate as it melts. When it is completely melted, remove from the heat and gradually stir in 10 more ounces of finely chopped milk chocolate, stirring until smooth. Dip the caramel squares in the warm chocolate using the instructions on pages 22–25. Place the dipped caramels on a parchment-lined pan and, if desired, gently sprinkle some cardamom on the top for decoration (make sure to add the cardamom before the chocolate coating dries).

Once cut, caramels should be stored in the resealable container in the refrigerator in order for them to keep their shape. Stored properly, caramels will keep for a month.

One of the world's oldest spices, cardamom is a staple in the cuisines of India and many other Southeast Asian countries. The Vikings were so struck by the spice, they brought it from Constantinople to Scandinavia, where it has become a key ingredient in many sweets.

Rum Vanilla Caramels

The addition of dark rum deepens and enriches these buttery vanilla caramels. To pump up the rum flavor, half is added at the beginning of the cooking process and half at the end.

Makes about 72 caramels.

(recipe continues on next page)

Rum Vanilla Caramels (continued)

YOU WILL NEED

Small bowl
5-quart saucepan with tall sides
Pastry brush and a small mug of
 warm water
Wooden spoon
Calibrated candy thermometer

9 X 9-inch pan, oiled and lined
 with parchment paper
Sharp knife
Bain marie
Fork or dipping tools
Resealable container for storage

INGREDIENTS

1 teaspoon vanilla extract
2 tablespoons rum extract
4 tablespoons dark rum, divided
2 cups sugar
1 cup light brown sugar,
 firmly packed
$1/2$ cup light corn syrup
$1/2$ cup honey
1 cup evaporated milk

2 cups heavy cream
$1/2$ cup unsalted butter,
 cut into pieces
Pinch of salt

30 ounces white chocolate, finely
 chopped and separated
10 ounces dark chocolate drizzle
 for decoration (optional)

Instructions:

In the small bowl, mix together the vanilla and rum extracts and 2 tablespoons of dark rum. Set aside.

In the saucepan, mix together the sugars, corn syrup, honey, evaporated milk, heavy cream, butter, salt, and remaining 2 tablespoons of dark rum. Place the saucepan on the stove over medium heat and stir with the wooden spoon until all the sugar is dissolved, the butter is melted, and the mixture is smooth. Increase the heat to medium high and let the mixture boil without stirring. Brush the sides of the saucepan regularly with the pastry brush dipped in warm water to keep the caramel from crystallizing.

Check the temperature regularly with your candy thermometer until it reaches 250°F (121°C). (Be patient as it will take at least 20 minutes or so.) Then remove the saucepan from the heat and add the vanilla/rum mixture, stirring thoroughly to blend. Pour the caramel into the prepared pan and let it cool for a few hours. When set, invert the caramel onto a new piece of parchment paper and cut it into squares with the sharp knife.

To make the chocolate coating, place 20 ounces of chopped white chocolate in the bain marie (bowl over a saucepan ¼ full of water). Heat the water over medium-low heat and gently stir the chocolate as it melts. When it is completely melted, remove from the heat and gradually stir in 10 more ounces of finely chopped white chocolate, stirring until smooth. Dip the caramel squares in the warm chocolate using the instructions on pages 22–25. Place the dipped caramels on a parchment-lined pan and, if desired, drizzle with a little dark chocolate as shown on pages 25–26 (make sure to add the drizzle after the chocolate coating dries).

Once cut, caramels should be stored in the resealable container in the refrigerator in order for them to keep their shape. Stored properly, caramels will keep for a month.

For the best flavor, make sure to use a good-quality dark rum. Spiced dark rum is another option if you prefer a little heat in your caramel.

Salted Vanilla Caramels

Americans have long had an infatuation with all things sweet and salty, so it's no surprise that salted caramels have grown so popular in recent years. The salt really complements the flavor of the vanilla caramel. The ones shown here have been dipped in dark chocolate and sprinkled with fleur de sel.

Makes about 72 caramels.

YOU WILL NEED

5-quart saucepan with tall sides
Pastry brush and a small mug of
  warm water
Wooden spoon
Calibrated candy thermometer
9 X 9-inch pan, oiled and lined
  with parchment paper

Sharp knife
Bain marie
Fork or dipping tools
Resealable container for storage

INGREDIENTS

2 cups sugar
1 cup light brown sugar,
  firmly packed
½ cup light corn syrup
½ cup honey
1 cup evaporated milk
2 cups heavy cream
½ cup unsalted butter, cut into pieces

2 teaspoons fleur de sel (or sea salt)
2 teaspoons vanilla extract

30 ounces bittersweet chocolate,
  finely chopped and divided
1 tablespoon fleur de sel or sea salt
  for decoration (optional)

Instructions:

In the saucepan, mix together the sugars, corn syrup, honey, evaporated milk, heavy cream, butter, and fleur de sel. Place the saucepan on the stove over medium heat and stir with the wooden spoon until all the sugar is dissolved, the butter is melted, and the mixture is smooth. Increase the heat to medium high and let the mixture boil without stirring. Brush the sides of the saucepan regularly with the pastry brush dipped in warm water to keep the caramel from crystallizing.

Check the temperature regularly with your candy thermometer until it reaches 250°F (121°C). (Be patient as it will take at least 20 minutes or so.) Then remove the saucepan from the heat and add the vanilla, stirring thoroughly to blend. Pour the caramel into the prepared pan and let it cool for a few hours. When set, invert the caramel onto a new piece of parchment paper and cut it into squares with the sharp knife.

(recipe continues on next page)

Salted Vanilla Caramels (continued)

To make the chocolate coating, place 20 ounces of chopped bittersweet chocolate in the bain marie (bowl over a saucepan ¼ full of water). Heat the water over medium-low heat and gently stir the chocolate as it melts. When it is completely melted, remove from the heat and gradually stir in 10 more ounces of finely chopped bittersweet chocolate, stirring until smooth. Dip the caramel squares in the warm chocolate using the instructions on pages 22–25. Place the dipped caramels on a parchment-lined pan and, if desired, gently sprinkle some salt on the top for decoration (make sure to add the salt before the chocolate coating dries).

Once cut, caramels should be stored in the resealable container in the refrigerator in order for them to keep their shape. Stored properly, caramels will keep for a month.

Be sure to use a coarse salt such as fleur de sel or sea salt and feel free to experiment with different varieties such as Himalayan pink salt or Celtic grey salt.

Ginger Vanilla Caramels

The fresh and tangy flavor of ginger adds a little spice to classic vanilla caramel. These are delicious on their own, but even more over-the-top when dipped in chocolate as are the ones shown here. We've dressed them up with a bit of crystallized ginger — it adds an extra flavor zing, looks decorative, and offers a clue to what's inside.

Makes about 72 caramels.

(recipe continues on next page)

Ginger Vanilla Caramels (continued)

YOU WILL NEED

Zester
Small strainer
2 small bowls
5-quart saucepan with tall sides
Pastry brush and a small mug of
    warm water

Wooden spoon
Calibrated candy thermometer
9 X 9-inch pan, oiled and lined
    with parchment paper
Sharp knife
Resealable container for storage

INGREDIENTS

2-inch piece of fresh ginger root,
    peeled
4 teaspoons vanilla extract
2/3 cup finely diced candied ginger
2 cups sugar
1 cup light brown sugar,
    firmly packed
1/2 cup light corn syrup
1/2 cup honey
1 cup evaporated milk

2 cups heavy cream
1/2 cup unsalted butter,
    cut into pieces
Pinch of salt

30 ounces milk chocolate, finely
    chopped and divided
Crystallized ginger pieces for
    decoration (optional)

Instructions:

With the zester, grate the peeled ginger root into the strainer placed over a small bowl. Press the ginger pulp firmly to the bottom of the strainer to get as much ginger juice as possible. Pour 4 teaspoons of the ginger juice into the second bowl and add the vanilla. Mix in the candied ginger and set aside.

In the saucepan, mix the sugars, corn syrup, honey, evaporated milk, heavy cream, butter, and salt, and place on the stove over medium heat. Stir with the wooden spoon until all the sugar is dissolved, the butter is melted, and the mixture is smooth. Increase the heat to medium high and let the mixture boil without stirring. Brush the sides of the saucepan regularly with the pastry brush dipped in warm water to keep the caramel from crystallizing.

Check the temperature regularly with your candy thermometer until it reaches 250°F (121°C). (Be patient as it will take at least 20 minutes or so.)

Then remove the saucepan from the heat and add the vanilla/ginger mix, stirring carefully to blend. Pour the caramel into the prepared pan and let it cool for a few hours. When set, invert the caramel onto a new piece of parchment paper and cut it in squares with the sharp knife.

To make the chocolate coating, place 20 ounces of the chopped milk chocolate in the bain marie (bowl over a saucepan $\frac{1}{4}$ full of water). Heat the water over medium-low heat and gently stir the chocolate as it melts. When it is completely melted, remove from the heat and gradually stir in 10 more ounces of finely chopped milk chocolate, stirring until smooth. Dip the caramel squares in the warm chocolate using the instructions on pages 22–25. Place the dipped caramels on a parchment-lined pan and, if desired, place 2 pieces of crystallized ginger on the top for decoration (make sure to add the ginger before the chocolate coating dries).

Once cut, caramels should be stored in the resealable container in the refrigerator in order for them to keep their shape. Stored properly, caramels will keep for a month.

In addition to tasting great, ginger has some health benefits. It has been used as a digestive aid for centuries and, when boiled in water, makes a soothing tonic for the common cold.

Chocolate Caramels

Classic Chocolate Caramels

Chocolate and caramel — two of the most sublime flavors mixed together. We'd like to see anyone resist these decadent treats. Note that the chocolate caramels tend to be a little denser and chewier than the vanilla and coffee caramels.

Makes about 72 caramels.

YOU WILL NEED

5-quart saucepan with tall sides
Pastry brush and a small mug of
  warm water
Wooden spoon
Calibrated candy thermometer

9 X 9-inch pan, oiled and lined
  with parchment paper
Sharp knife
Resealable container for storage

INGREDIENTS

2 cups sugar
1 cup light brown sugar,
  firmly packed
1/2 cup light corn syrup
1/2 cup honey
1 cup evaporated milk
2 cups heavy cream

1/2 cup unsalted butter,
  cut into pieces
Pinch of salt
4 ounces unsweetened chocolate,
  chopped fine
2 teaspoons vanilla extract

Instructions:

In the saucepan, mix together the sugar, brown sugar, corn syrup, honey, evaporated milk, heavy cream, butter, and salt. Place the saucepan on the stove over medium heat and stir with the wooden spoon until all the sugar is dissolved, the butter is melted, and the mixture is smooth. Increase the heat to medium high and let the mixture boil without stirring. Brush the sides of the saucepan regularly with the pastry brush dipped in warm water to keep the caramel from crystallizing.

Check the temperature regularly with your candy thermometer until it reaches 225°F (107°C). (Be patient as it will take at least 20 minutes or so.) Then carefully add the chopped chocolate. Stir gently a few times and then brush the sides of the saucepan. When the candy thermometer reaches 248°F (120°C), remove the saucepan from the heat and add the vanilla, stirring thoroughly to blend. Pour the caramel into the prepared pan and let it cool for a few hours. When set, invert the caramel onto a new piece of parchment paper and cut it into squares with the sharp knife.

Once cut, caramels should be stored in the resealable container in the refrigerator in order for them to keep their shape. Stored properly, caramels will keep for a month.

Mayan Chocolate Caramels

For a more exotic twist, we're heading south of the border. We've combined spices such as cinnamon, cloves, and chili powder with cocoa, resulting in a traditional Mexican-flavored treat. For a spicier version of these caramels, you may want to add more chili powder.

Makes about 72 caramels.

YOU WILL NEED

Small mixing bowl
5-quart saucepan with tall sides
Pastry brush and a small mug of
    warm water
Wooden spoon

Calibrated candy thermometer
9 X 9-inch pan, oiled and lined
    with parchment paper
Sharp knife
Resealable container for storage

INGREDIENTS

2 teaspoons vanilla extract
$1/2$ teaspoon freshly grated nutmeg
$1/4$ teaspoon ground cloves
1 teaspoon cinnamon powder
Generous pinch of chili powder (to
    taste)
2 cups sugar
1 cup light brown sugar,
    firmly packed

$1/2$ cup light corn syrup
$1/2$ cup honey
1 cup evaporated milk
2 cups heavy cream
$1/2$ cup unsalted butter,
    cut into pieces
Pinch of salt
4 ounces unsweetened chocolate,
    chopped fine

Instructions:

In the small mixing bowl, mix together the vanilla, nutmeg, cloves, cinnamon, and chili powder. Set aside. In the saucepan, mix together the sugars, corn syrup, honey, evaporated milk, heavy cream, butter, and salt. Place the saucepan on the stove over medium heat and stir with the wooden spoon until all the sugar is dissolved, the butter is melted, and the mixture is smooth. Increase the heat to medium high and let the mixture boil without stirring. Brush the sides of the saucepan regularly with the pastry brush dipped in warm water to keep the caramel from crystallizing.

Check the temperature regularly with your candy thermometer until it reaches 225°F (107°C). (Be patient as it will take at least 20 minutes or so.) Then add the chopped chocolate. Stir gently a few times and then carefully brush the sides of the saucepan. When the candy thermometer reaches 248°F (120°C), remove the saucepan from the heat and add the vanilla/spice mixture, stirring thoroughly to blend. Pour the caramel into the prepared pan and let it cool for a few hours. When set, invert the caramel onto a new piece of parchment paper and cut it into squares with the sharp knife.

Once cut, caramels should be stored in the resealable container in the refrigerator in order for them to keep their shape. Stored properly, caramels will keep for a month.

Almond Chocolate Caramels

Almonds, chocolate, and caramel share a long and happy history. Like peanut butter and jelly, they just seem to go together. The crunchiness of the nuts, the chewiness of caramel, and the sweetness of the chocolate are a delectable combination.

Makes about 72 caramels.

YOU WILL NEED

5-quart saucepan with tall sides
Pastry brush and a small mug of
    warm water
Wooden spoon
Calibrated candy thermometer

9 X 9-inch pan, oiled and lined
    with parchment paper
Sharp knife
Bain marie
Fork or dipping tools
Resealable container for storage

INGREDIENTS

2 cups sugar
1 cup light brown sugar,
    firmly packed
1/2 cup light corn syrup
1/2 cup honey
1 cup evaporated milk
2 cups heavy cream
1/2 cup unsalted butter, cut into pieces
Pinch of salt

4 ounces unsweetened chocolate,
    chopped fine
2 teaspoons almond extract
1 cup almonds, chopped and toasted

30 ounces bittersweet chocolate,
    finely chopped and divided
Almond halves for decorating
    (optional)

Instructions:

In the saucepan, mix together the sugars, corn syrup, honey, evaporated milk, heavy cream, butter, and salt. Place the saucepan on the stove over medium heat and stir with the wooden spoon until all the sugar is dissolved, the butter is melted, and the mixture is smooth. Increase the heat to medium high and let the mixture boil without stirring. Brush the sides of the saucepan regularly with the pastry brush dipped in warm water to keep the caramel from crystallizing.

Check the temperature regularly with your candy thermometer until it reaches 225°F (107°C). (Be patient as it will take at least 20 minutes or so.) Then add the chopped unsweetened chocolate. Stir gently a few times and then carefully brush the sides of the saucepan. When the candy thermometer reaches 248°F (120°C), remove the saucepan from the heat and add the almond extract and chopped almonds, stirring thoroughly to blend. Pour the caramel into the prepared pan and let it cool for a few hours. When set, invert the caramel onto a new piece of parchment paper and cut it into squares with the sharp knife.

(recipe continues on next page)

Almond Chocolate Caramels (continued)

To make the chocolate coating, place 20 ounces of the chopped bittersweet chocolate in the bain marie (bowl over a saucepan $\frac{1}{4}$ full of water). Heat the water over medium-low heat and gently stir the chocolate as it melts. When it is completely melted, remove from the heat and gradually stir in 10 more ounces of finely chopped bittersweet chocolate, stirring until smooth. Dip the caramel squares in the warm chocolate using the instructions on pages 22–25. Place the dipped caramels on a parchment-lined pan and, if desired, gently place an almond half on the top for decoration (make sure to add the almond before the chocolate coating dries).

Once cut, caramels should be stored in the resealable container in the refrigerator in order for them to keep their shape. Stored properly, caramels will keep for a month.

Delicious and nutritious, almonds have been cultivated for thousands of years. In many cultures they are thought to represent good fortune.

Bananas Foster Chocolate Caramels

Those who enjoy the classic dessert Bananas Foster will go bananas for these caramels. To infuse the caramel with a pure banana flavor, we added freeze-dried banana chips, which had been ground to a fine powder.

Makes about 72 caramels.

(recipe continues on next page)

Bananas Foster Chocolate Caramels (continued)

YOU WILL NEED

5-quart saucepan with tall sides
Pastry brush and a small mug of
  warm water
Wooden spoon
Calibrated candy thermometer

9 X 9-inch pan, oiled and
  lined with parchment paper
Sharp knife
Bain marie
Fork or dipping tools
Resealable container for storage

INGREDIENTS

2 cups sugar
1 cup light brown sugar, firmly packed
1/2 cup light corn syrup
1/2 cup honey
1 cup evaporated milk
2 cups heavy cream
1/2 cup unsalted butter, cut into pieces
Pinch of salt
3 tablespoons dark rum, divided

4 ounces unsweetened chocolate,
  chopped fine
1 cup freeze-dried banana chips,
  ground to a fine powder
1 teaspoon rum extract

30 ounces bittersweet chocolate,
  finely chopped and divided
Banana chips for decorating
  (optional)

Instructions:

In the saucepan, mix together the sugars, corn syrup, honey, evaporated milk, heavy cream, butter, salt, and 2 tablespoons of dark rum. Place the saucepan on the stove over medium heat and stir with the wooden spoon until all the sugar is dissolved, the butter is melted, and the mixture is smooth. Increase the heat to medium high and let the mixture boil without stirring. Brush the sides of the saucepan regularly with the pastry brush dipped in warm water to keep the caramel from crystallizing.

Check the temperature regularly with your candy thermometer until it reaches 225°F (107°C). (Be patient as it will take at least 20 minutes or so.) Then add the chopped unsweetened chocolate. Stir gently a few times and then carefully brush the sides of the saucepan. When the candy thermometer reaches 248°F (120°C), remove the saucepan from the heat and add the ground banana chips, rum extract, and remaining 1 tablespoon of dark rum, stirring thoroughly to blend. Pour the caramel into the prepared pan and let it cool for a few hours. When set, invert the caramel onto a new piece of parchment paper and cut it into squares with the sharp knife.

To make the chocolate coating, place 20 ounces of the chopped bittersweet chocolate in the bain marie (bowl over a saucepan $\frac{1}{4}$ full of water). Heat the water over medium-low heat and gently stir the chocolate as it melts. When it is completely melted, remove from the heat and gradually stir in 10 more ounces of finely chopped bittersweet chocolate, stirring until smooth. Dip the caramel squares in the warm chocolate using the instructions on pages 22–25. Place the dipped caramels on a parchment-lined pan and, if desired, gently place a banana chip on the top for decoration (make sure to add the chip before the chocolate coating dries).

Once cut, caramels should be stored in the resealable container in the refrigerator in order for them to keep their shape. Stored properly, caramels will keep for a month.

Decorating these caramels with banana chips is a great way to clue others in to their flavor. If you don't have banana chips on hand, you could also sprinkle the top with a little cinnamon — it won't provide much of a hint, but it will certainly taste delicious!

Coconut Chocolate Caramels

From the number of popular candy bars and cookies featuring these ingredients, it seems pretty clear that coconut, chocolate, and caramel are a winning combination. The caramels here provide just the right amount of chewy, crunchy texture and sweet tropical flavor.

Makes about 72 caramels.

YOU WILL NEED

5-quart saucepan with tall sides
Pastry brush and a small mug of
  warm water
Wooden spoon
Calibrated candy thermometer

9 X 9-inch pan, oiled and lined
  with parchment paper
Sharp knife
Bain marie
Fork or dipping tools
Resealable container for storage

INGREDIENTS

2 cups sugar
1 cup light brown sugar,
  firmly packed
$1/2$ cup light corn syrup
$1/2$ cup honey
1 cup evaporated milk
2 cups heavy cream
$1/2$ cup unsalted butter,
  cut into pieces
Pinch of salt

4 ounces unsweetened chocolate,
  chopped fine
2 teaspoons vanilla extract
4 teaspoons coconut extract
$1 1/2$ cups sweetened, shredded coconut

30 ounces bittersweet chocolate,
  finely chopped and divided
Sweetened, shredded coconut for
  decorating (optional)

Instructions:

In the saucepan, mix together the sugars, corn syrup, honey, evaporated milk, heavy cream, butter, and salt. Place the saucepan on the stove over medium heat and stir with the wooden spoon until all the sugar is dissolved, the butter is melted, and the mixture is smooth. Increase the heat to medium high and let the mixture boil without stirring. Brush the sides of the saucepan regularly with the pastry brush dipped in warm water to keep the caramel from crystallizing.

Check the temperature regularly with your candy thermometer until it reaches 225°F (107°C). (Be patient as it will take at least 20 minutes or so.) Then add the chopped unsweetened chocolate. Stir gently a few times and then carefully brush the sides of the saucepan. When the candy thermometer reaches 248°F (120°C), remove the saucepan from the heat and add the vanilla and coconut extracts, stirring thoroughly to blend. Add the coconut and mix well. Pour the caramel into the prepared pan and let it set for a few hours. When set, invert the caramel onto a new piece of parchment paper and cut it into squares with the sharp knife.

(recipe continues on next page)

Coconut Chocolate Caramels *(continued)*

To make the chocolate coating, place 20 ounces of the chopped bittersweet chocolate in the bain marie (bowl over a saucepan ¼ full of water). Heat the water over medium-low heat and gently stir the chocolate as it melts. When it is completely melted, remove from the heat and gradually stir in 10 more ounces of finely chopped bittersweet chocolate, stirring until smooth. Dip the caramel squares in the warm chocolate using the instructions on pages 22–25. Place the dipped caramels on a parchment-lined pan and, if desired, gently sprinkle some coconut on the top for decoration (make sure to add the coconut before the chocolate coating dries).

Once cut, caramels should be stored in the resealable container in the refrigerator in order for them to keep their shape. Stored properly, caramels will keep for a month.

In some places coconut is called "the tree of life" due to its versatility and the fact that all of its parts can be utilized in some manner.

Mint Chocolate Caramels

These mint chocolate caramels are a chewy version of those wonderful chocolate mint cookies sold by young girls in green uniforms. And just like those cookies, these cool, refreshing, minty indulgences are highly addictive.

Makes about 72 caramels.

(recipe continues on next page)

Mint Chocolate Caramels (continued)

YOU WILL NEED

5-quart saucepan with tall sides
Pastry brush and a small mug of
    warm water
Wooden spoon
Calibrated candy thermometer

9 X 9-inch pan, oiled and lined
    with parchment paper
Sharp knife
Bain marie
Fork or dipping tools
Resealable container for storage

INGREDIENTS

2 cups sugar
1 cup light brown sugar,
    firmly packed
1/2 cup light corn syrup
1/2 cup honey
1 cup evaporated milk
2 cups heavy cream
1/2 cup unsalted butter, cut into pieces
Pinch of salt

4 ounces unsweetened chocolate,
    chopped fine
3 teaspoons peppermint extract

30 ounces bittersweet chocolate,
    finely chopped and divided
Crushed peppermint candies for
    decoration (optional)

Instructions:

In the saucepan, mix together the sugars, corn syrup, honey, evaporated milk, heavy cream, butter, and salt. Place the saucepan on the stove over medium heat and stir with the wooden spoon until all the sugar is dissolved, the butter is melted, and the mixture is smooth. Increase the heat to medium high and let the mixture boil without stirring. Brush the sides of the saucepan regularly with the pastry brush dipped in warm water to keep the caramel from crystallizing.

Check the temperature regularly with your candy thermometer until it reaches 225°F (107°C). (Be patient as it will take at least 20 minutes or so.) Then add the chopped unsweetened chocolate. Stir gently a few times and then carefully brush the sides of the saucepan. When the candy thermometer reaches 248°F (120°C), remove the saucepan from the heat and add the peppermint extract, stirring thoroughly to blend. Pour the caramel into the prepared pan and let it cool for a few hours. When set, invert the caramel onto a new piece of parchment paper and cut it into squares with the sharp knife.

To make the chocolate coating, place 20 ounces of the chopped bittersweet chocolate in the bain marie (bowl over a saucepan ¼ full of water). Heat the water over medium-low heat and gently stir the chocolate as it melts. When it is completely melted, remove from the heat and gradually stir in 10 more ounces of finely chopped bittersweet chocolate, stirring until smooth. Dip the caramel squares in the warm chocolate using the instructions on pages 22–25. Place the dipped caramels on a parchment-lined pan and, if desired, gently sprinkle some crushed peppermint candies on the top for decoration (make sure to add the peppermint candies before the chocolate coating dries).

Once cut, caramels should be stored in the resealable container in the refrigerator in order for them to keep their shape. Stored properly, caramels will keep for a month.

Since antiquity, mint has been known for its culinary, medicinal, and aromatic properties. There is even a Greek myth based on the herb in which a nymph named Minthe is turned into a plant by a jealous Persephone.

Orange Chocolate Caramels

Candied orange peel adds a wonderful texture and an extra dose of orange flavor to these chocolate caramels. The addition of Cointreau only intensifies the citrus taste.

Makes about 72 caramels.

YOU WILL NEED

5-quart saucepan with tall sides
Pastry brush and a small mug of
	warm water
Wooden spoon
Calibrated candy thermometer

9 X 9-inch pan, oiled and lined
	with parchment paper
Sharp knife
Bain marie
Fork or dipping tools
Resealable container for storage

INGREDIENTS

2 cups sugar
1 cup light brown sugar,
	firmly packed
$\frac{1}{2}$ cup light corn syrup
$\frac{1}{2}$ cup honey
1 cup evaporated milk
2 cups heavy cream
4 tablespoons unsalted butter,
	cut into pieces
Pinch of salt

4 tablespoons Cointreau or Grand
	Marnier, divided
4 ounces unsweetened chocolate,
	chopped fine
2 teaspoons orange zest
1$\frac{1}{2}$ cups chopped candied
	orange peel

30 ounces milk chocolate, finely
	chopped and divided
Small slices of candied orange peel
	for decoration (optional)

Instructions:

In the saucepan, mix together the sugars, corn syrup, honey, evaporated milk, heavy cream, butter, salt, and 2 tablespoons of Cointreau or Grand Marnier. Place the saucepan on the stove over medium heat and stir with the wooden spoon until all the sugar is dissolved, the butter is melted, and the mixture is smooth. Increase the heat to medium high and let the mixture boil without stirring. Brush the sides of the saucepan regularly with the pastry brush dipped in warm water to keep the caramel from crystallizing.

Check the temperature regularly with your candy thermometer until it reaches 225°F (107°C). (Be patient as it will take at least 20 minutes or so.) Then add the chopped unsweetened chocolate. Stir gently a few times and then carefully brush the sides of the saucepan. When the candy thermometer reaches 248°F (120°C), remove the saucepan from the heat and add the zest and orange peel, stirring thoroughly to blend. Pour the caramel into the prepared pan and let it cool for a few hours. When set, invert the caramel onto a new piece of parchment paper and cut it into squares with the sharp knife.

(recipe continues on next page)

Orange Chocolate Caramels (continued)

To make the chocolate coating, place 20 ounces of the chopped milk chocolate in the bain marie (bowl over a saucepan ¼ full of water). Heat the water over medium-low heat and gently stir the chocolate as it melts. When it is completely melted, remove from the heat and gradually stir in 10 more ounces of finely chopped milk chocolate, stirring until smooth. Dip the caramel squares in the warm chocolate using the instructions on pages 22–25. Place the dipped caramels on a parchment-lined pan and, if desired, gently place some sliced candied orange peel on the top for decoration (make sure to add the orange peel before the chocolate coating dries).

Once cut, caramels should be stored in the resealable container in the refrigerator in order for them to keep their shape. Stored properly, caramels will keep for a month.

You can find candied orange peel in specialty food stores or online. It adds wonderful texture to the caramels and makes splendid decorations.

Peanut Butter Chocolate Caramels

These caramels are reminiscent of old-fashioned peanut chews. All-natural peanut butter gives them a rich peanut flavor that is further embellished by the addition of crunchy roasted peanuts.

Makes about 72 caramels.

(recipe continues on next page)

Peanut Butter Chocolate Caramels (continued)

YOU WILL NEED

5-quart saucepan with tall sides
Pastry brush and a small mug of
   warm water
Wooden spoon
Calibrated candy thermometer

9 X 9-inch pan, oiled and lined
   with parchment paper
Sharp knife
Bain marie
Fork or dipping tools
Resealable container for storage

INGREDIENTS

2 cups sugar
1 cup light brown sugar,
   firmly packed
½ cup light corn syrup
½ cup honey
1 cup evaporated milk
2 cups heavy cream
½ cup unsalted butter, cut into pieces
Pinch of salt
4 ounces unsweetened chocolate,
   chopped fine

1 teaspoon vanilla extract
2 tablespoons smooth natural peanut butter (not hydrogenated)
1 cup roasted peanuts, chopped

30 ounces bittersweet chocolate,
   finely chopped and divided
Peanut halves for decorating
   (optional)

Instructions:

In the saucepan, mix together the sugars, corn syrup, honey, evaporated milk, heavy cream, butter, and salt. Place the saucepan on the stove over medium heat and stir with the wooden spoon until all the sugar is dissolved, the butter is melted, and the mixture is smooth. Increase the heat to medium high and let the mixture boil without stirring. Brush the sides of the saucepan regularly with the pastry brush dipped in warm water to keep the caramel from crystallizing.

Check the temperature regularly with your candy thermometer until it reaches 225°F (107°C). (Be patient as it will take at least 20 minutes or so.) Then add the chopped unsweetened chocolate. Stir gently a few times and then carefully brush the sides of the saucepan. When the candy thermometer reaches 248°F (120°C), remove the saucepan from the heat and add the vanilla extract, peanut butter, and chopped peanuts, stirring thoroughly to blend. Pour the caramel into the prepared pan and let it cool for a few hours. When set, invert the caramel onto a new piece of parchment paper and cut it into squares with the sharp knife.

To make the chocolate coating, place 20 ounces of the chopped bittersweet chocolate in the bain marie (bowl over a saucepan ¼ full of water). Heat the water over medium-low heat and gently stir the chocolate as it melts. When it is completely melted, remove from the heat and gradually stir in 10 more ounces of finely chopped bittersweet chocolate, stirring until smooth. Dip the caramel squares in the warm chocolate using the instructions on pages 22–25. Place the dipped caramels on a parchment-lined pan and, if desired, gently place a peanut half on the top for decoration (make sure to add the peanut half before the chocolate coating dries).

Once cut, caramels should be stored in the resealable container in the refrigerator in order for them to keep their shape. Stored properly, caramels will keep for a month.

Introduced in 1917, high-protein peanut chews were originally used by the U.S. military as a ration bar during World War I.

Coffee Caramels

Classic Coffee Caramels

The intense, sophisticated flavor of these creamy coffee caramels provides the perfect ending to a leisurely afternoon lunch. Then again, they're a great pick-me-up any time of day. For best results use a good-quality instant coffee or, even better, an instant espresso powder.

Makes about 72 caramels.

YOU WILL NEED

Small mixing bowl
5-quart saucepan with tall sides
Pastry brush and a small mug of
    warm water
Wooden spoon

Calibrated candy thermometer
9 X 9-inch pan, oiled and lined
    with parchment paper
Sharp knife
Resealable container for storage

INGREDIENTS

2 teaspoons vanilla extract
2 tablespoons instant coffee or
    espresso powder
2 cups sugar
1 cup light brown sugar,
    firmly packed
$\frac{1}{2}$ cup light corn syrup

$\frac{1}{2}$ cup honey
1 cup evaporated milk
2 cups heavy cream
$\frac{1}{2}$ cup unsalted butter,
    cut into pieces
Pinch of salt

Instructions:

In the small bowl, mix the vanilla extract with the instant coffee or espresso powder and set aside.

In the saucepan, mix together the sugars, corn syrup, honey, evaporated milk, heavy cream, butter, and salt. Place the saucepan on the stove over medium heat and stir with the wooden spoon until all the sugar is dissolved, the butter is melted, and the mixture is smooth. Increase the heat to medium high and let the mixture boil without stirring. Brush the sides of the saucepan regularly with the pastry brush dipped in warm water to keep the caramel from crystallizing.

Check the temperature regularly with your candy thermometer until it reaches 250°F (121°C). (Be patient as it will take at least 20 minutes or so.) Then remove the saucepan from the heat and add the vanilla/coffee mixture, stirring carefully to blend. Pour the caramel into the prepared pan and let it cool for a few hours. When set, invert the caramel onto a new piece of parchment paper and cut it into squares with the sharp knife.

Once cut, caramels should be stored in the resealable container in the refrigerator in order for them to keep their shape. Stored properly, caramels will keep for a month.

Maple Bacon Coffee Caramels

We like to call these sweet and savory little morsels the "breakfast of champions." Though maybe not the healthiest way to start the day, these caramels will certainly put anyone in a great mood.

Makes about 72 caramels.

YOU WILL NEED

Small bowl
5-quart saucepan with tall sides
Pastry brush and a small mug of warm water
Wooden spoon

Calibrated candy thermometer
9 X 9-inch pan, oiled and lined with parchment paper
Sharp knife
Resealable container for storage

INGREDIENTS

1 pound bacon, cooked until crisp and crumbled into tiny pieces, divided
2 teaspoons vanilla extract
2 tablespoons instant coffee or espresso powder
2 cups sugar
1 cup light brown sugar, firmly packed

^{1}/₂ cup light corn syrup
^{1}/₂ cup pure maple syrup
1 cup evaporated milk
2 cups heavy cream
^{1}/₂ cup unsalted butter, cut into pieces
Pinch of salt

Instructions:

In the small bowl, mix half the bacon bits with the vanilla and instant coffee or espresso powder and set aside.

In the saucepan, mix together the sugars, corn syrup, maple syrup, evaporated milk, heavy cream, butter, and salt. Place the saucepan on the stove over medium heat and stir with the wooden spoon until all the sugar is dissolved, the butter is melted, and the mixture is smooth. Increase the heat to medium high and let the mixture boil without stirring. Brush the sides of the saucepan regularly with the pastry brush dipped in warm water to keep the caramel from crystallizing.

Check the temperature regularly with your candy thermometer until it reaches 250°F (121°C). (Be patient as it will take at least 20 minutes or so.) Then remove the saucepan from the heat and add the bacon/vanilla/coffee mixture, stirring thoroughly to blend. Pour the caramel into the prepared pan. Sprinkle the remaining bacon bits on top and let it cool for a few hours. When set, invert the caramel onto a new piece of parchment paper and cut it into squares with the sharp knife.

Once cut, caramels should be stored in the resealable container in the refrigerator in order for them to keep their shape. Stored properly, caramels will keep for a week.

Hazelnut Frangelico Coffee Caramels

While coffee caramels are sophisticated on their own, the addition of Frangelico, a hazelnut-flavored liqueur, takes them to a new height. Chopped toasted hazelnuts give the confection the most wonderful chewy and crunchy texture.

Makes about 72 caramels.

YOU WILL NEED

Small mixing bowl
5-quart saucepan with tall sides
Pastry brush and a small mug of
    warm water
Wooden spoon

Calibrated candy thermometer
9 X 9-inch pan, oiled and lined
    with parchment paper
Sharp knife
Resealable container for storage

INGREDIENTS

1 teaspoon vanilla extract
2 tablespoons instant coffee or
    espresso powder
2 tablespoons Frangelico liqueur
¾ cup toasted hazelnuts,
    coarsely chopped
2 cups sugar
1 cup light brown sugar,
    firmly packed

½ cup light corn syrup
½ cup honey
1 cup evaporated milk
2 cups heavy cream
½ cup unsalted butter, cut into pieces
Pinch of salt

Instructions:

In the small bowl, mix the vanilla extract with the instant coffee or espresso powder, Frangelico, and hazelnuts and set aside.

In the saucepan, mix together the sugars, corn syrup, honey, evaporated milk, heavy cream, butter, and salt. Place the saucepan on the stove over medium heat and stir with the wooden spoon until all the sugar is dissolved, the butter is melted, and the mixture is smooth. Increase the heat to medium high and let the mixture boil without stirring. Brush the sides of the saucepan regularly with the pastry brush dipped in warm water to keep the caramel from crystallizing.

Check the temperature regularly with your candy thermometer until it reaches 250°F (121°C). (Be patient as it will take at least 20 minutes or so.) Then remove the saucepan from the heat and add the vanilla/coffee mixture, stirring thoroughly to blend. Pour the caramel into the prepared pan and let it cool for a few hours. When set, invert the caramel onto a new piece of parchment paper and cut it into squares with the sharp knife.

Once cut, caramels should be stored in the resealable container in the refrigerator in order for them to keep their shape. Stored properly, caramels will keep for a month.

Anise Coffee Caramels

In Italy, Sambuca, an anise-flavored liqueur, is often served with three coffee beans dropped in to represent health, happiness, and prosperity. These anise coffee caramels were inspired by this traditional combination. Salute.

Makes about 72 caramels.

YOU WILL NEED

Small bowl
5-quart saucepan with tall sides
Pastry brush and a small mug of
    warm water
Wooden spoon
Calibrated candy thermometer

9 X 9-inch pan, oiled and lined
    with parchment paper
Sharp knife
Bain marie
Fork or dipping tools
Resealable container for storage

INGREDIENTS

2 tablespoons anise extract
2 tablespoons instant coffee or
    espresso powder
2 cups sugar
1 cup light brown sugar, firmly
    packed
1/2 cup light corn syrup
1/2 cup honey
1 cup evaporated milk

2 cups heavy cream
1/2 cup unsalted butter, cut into
    pieces
Pinch of salt

30 ounces milk chocolate, finely
    chopped and divided
Chocolate espresso beans for
    decoration (optional)

Instructions:

In the small bowl, mix the anise extract with the instant coffee or espresso powder and set aside.

In the saucepan, mix together the sugars, corn syrup, honey, evaporated milk, heavy cream, butter, and salt. Place the saucepan on the stove over medium heat and stir with the wooden spoon until all the sugar is dissolved, the butter is melted, and the mixture is smooth. Increase the heat to medium high and let the mixture boil without stirring. Brush the sides of the saucepan regularly with the pastry brush dipped in warm water to keep the caramel from crystallizing.

Check the temperature regularly with your candy thermometer until it reaches 250°F (121°C). (Be patient as it will take at least 20 minutes or so.) Then remove the saucepan from the heat and add the anise/espresso mixture, stirring thoroughly to blend. Pour the caramel into the prepared pan and let it cool for a few hours. When set, invert the caramel onto a new piece of parchment paper and cut it into squares with the sharp knife.

(recipe continues on next page)

Anise Coffee Caramels (continued)

To make the chocolate coating, place 20 ounces of the chopped milk chocolate in the bain marie (bowl over a saucepan ¼ full of water). Heat the water over medium-low heat and gently stir the chocolate as it melts. When it is completely melted, remove from the heat and gradually stir in 10 more ounces of finely chopped milk chocolate, stirring until smooth. Dip the caramel squares in the warm chocolate using the instructions on pages 22–25. Place the dipped caramels on a parchment-lined pan and, if desired, gently place a chocolate espresso bean on the top for decoration (make sure to add the espresso bean before the chocolate coating dries).

Once cut, caramels should be stored in the resealable container in the refrigerator in order for them to keep their shape. Stored properly, caramels will keep for a month.

Distinguished by its licorice-like flavor, anise has long been used as a digestive aid as well as a natural breath freshener.

Bourbon Pecan Coffee Caramels

These caramels feature three ingredients — bourbon, pecans, and coffee — that simply bring out the best in each other. Dipped in white chocolate and decorated with pecan halves, these boozy morsels are sinfully good.

Makes about 72 caramels.

(recipe continues on next page)

Bourbon Pecan Coffee Caramels (continued)

YOU WILL NEED

2 small bowls
5-quart saucepan with tall sides
Pastry brush and a small mug of
    warm water
Wooden spoon
Calibrated candy thermometer

9 X 9-inch pan, oiled and lined
    with parchment paper
Sharp knife
Bain marie
Fork or dipping tools
Resealable container for storage

INGREDIENTS

1 cup plus 3 tablespoons bourbon,
    divided
2 tablespoons instant coffee or
    espresso powder
1½ cups chopped pecans
2 cups sugar
1 cup light brown sugar,
    firmly packed
1 cup honey

1 cup evaporated milk
2 cups heavy cream
½ cup unsalted butter, cut into pieces
Pinch of salt

30 ounces white chocolate, finely
    chopped and divided
Pecan halves for decorating (optional)

Instructions:

Place 1 tablespoon of bourbon with the instant coffee or espresso powder in one small bowl and gently mix. In another bowl mix together the chopped pecans with the remaining 2 tablespoons of bourbon. Set aside.

In the saucepan, mix together the sugars, honey, evaporated milk, heavy cream, butter, salt, and 1 cup of the bourbon. Place the saucepan on the stove over medium heat and stir with the wooden spoon until all the sugar is dissolved, the butter is melted, and the mixture is smooth. Increase the heat to medium high and let the mixture boil without stirring. Brush the sides of the saucepan regularly with the pastry brush dipped in warm water to keep the caramel from crystallizing.

Check the temperature regularly with your candy thermometer until it reaches 250°F (121°C). (Be patient as it will take at least 20 minutes or so.) Then remove the saucepan from the heat and add the bourbon/coffee mixture, stirring thoroughly to blend. Add the chopped pecan/bourbon mix and stir to blend. Pour the caramel into the prepared pan and let it cool for a few hours. When set, invert the caramel onto a new piece of parchment paper and cut it into squares with the sharp knife.

To make the chocolate coating, place 20 ounces of the chopped white chocolate in the bain marie (bowl over a saucepan ¼ full of water). Heat the water over medium-low heat and gently stir the chocolate as it melts. When it is completely melted, remove from the heat and gradually stir in 10 more ounces of finely chopped white chocolate, stirring until smooth. Dip the caramel squares in the warm chocolate using the instructions on pages 22–25. Place the dipped caramels on a parchment-lined pan and, if desired, gently place a pecan half on the top for decoration (make sure to add the pecan before the chocolate coating dries).

Once cut, caramels should be stored in the resealable container in the refrigerator in order for them to keep their shape. Stored properly, caramels will keep for a month.

Bourbon is a type of whiskey originally produced in Bourbon County, Kentucky. In order to be called a true bourbon, whiskey must contain between 51 and 79 percent Indian corn and it must be aged for at least 2 years in a new oak barrel that has been charred on the inside.

Brandy Coffee Caramels

These chewy delights capture the soothing, intoxicating warmth of brandy-spiked coffee. Heightened by the sweet flavor and sublime texture of caramel, they're a perfect treat for a cold winter evening by the fire.

Makes about 72 caramels.

YOU WILL NEED

Small mixing bowl
5-quart saucepan with tall sides
Pastry brush and a small mug of
   warm water
Wooden spoon
Calibrated candy thermometer

9 X 9-inch pan, oiled and lined
   with parchment paper
Sharp knife
Bain marie
Fork or dipping tools
Resealable container for storage

INGREDIENTS

1 cup plus 2 tablespoons Cognac
   or similar brandy, divided
2 tablespoons instant coffee or
   espresso powder
2 cups sugar
1 cup light brown sugar,
   firmly packed
1 cup honey
1 cup evaporated milk

2 cups heavy cream
1/2 cup unsalted butter, cut into pieces
Pinch of salt

30 ounces milk chocolate, finely
   chopped and divided
10 ounces white chocolate
   for drizzling (optional)

Instructions:

In the small bowl, mix together 2 tablespoons of brandy with the instant coffee or espresso powder and set aside.

In the saucepan, mix together the sugars, honey, evaporated milk, heavy cream, butter, salt, and remaining 1 cup of brandy. Place the saucepan on the stove over medium heat and stir with the wooden spoon until all the sugar is dissolved, the butter is melted, and the mixture is smooth. Increase the heat to medium high and let the mixture boil without stirring. Brush the sides of the saucepan regularly with the pastry brush dipped in warm water to keep the caramel from crystallizing.

Check the temperature regularly with your candy thermometer until it reaches 250°F (121°C). (Be patient as it will take at least 20 minutes or so.) Then remove the saucepan from the heat and add the brandy/coffee mixture, stirring thoroughly to blend. Pour the caramel into the prepared pan and let it cool for a few hours. When set, invert the caramel onto a new piece of parchment paper and cut it into squares with the sharp knife.

(recipe continues on next page)

To make the chocolate coating, place 20 ounces of the chopped milk chocolate in the bain marie (bowl over a saucepan ¼ full of water). Heat the water over medium-low heat and gently stir the chocolate as it melts. When it is completely melted, remove from the heat and gradually stir in 10 more ounces of finely chopped milk chocolate, stirring until smooth. Dip the caramel squares in the warm chocolate using the instructions on pages 22–25. Place the dipped caramels on a parchment-lined pan and, if desired, gently drizzle white chocolate as shown on pages 25–26 (make sure to add the drizzle after the chocolate coating dries).

Once cut, caramels should be stored in the resealable container in the refrigerator in order for them to keep their shape. Stored properly, caramels will keep for a month.

The Café Royal is a popular after-dinner drink in France. Featuring coffee, brandy, sugar, and cream, the warm drink provided inspiration for these Brandy Coffee Caramels.

Cinnamon Spice Coffee Caramels

"Sugar and spice and everything nice" is a good way to describe
these yummy caramels. Covered in white chocolate and sprinkled with
cinnamon, these are a delight for the eyes as well as the taste buds.

Makes about 72 caramels.

(recipe continues on next page)

Cinnamon Spice Coffee Caramels (continued)

YOU WILL NEED

Small bowl
5-quart saucepan with tall sides
Pastry brush and a small mug of
  warm water
Wooden spoon
Calibrated candy thermometer

9 X 9-inch pan, oiled and lined
  with parchment paper
Sharp knife
Bain marie
Fork or dipping tools
Resealable container for storage

INGREDIENTS

1 tablespoon vanilla extract
2 tablespoons instant coffee or
  espresso powder
3 teaspoons cinnamon
2 cups sugar
1 cup light brown sugar,
  firmly packed
1 cup honey

1 cup evaporated milk
2 cups heavy cream
½ cup unsalted butter, cut into pieces
Pinch of salt

30 ounces white chocolate, finely
  chopped and divided
Cinnamon for decoration

Instructions:

In the small bowl, mix the vanilla, instant coffee or espresso powder, and cinnamon together and set aside.

In the saucepan, mix together the sugars, honey, evaporated milk, heavy cream, butter, and salt. Place the saucepan on the stove over medium heat and stir with the wooden spoon until all the sugar is dissolved, the butter is melted, and the mixture is smooth. Increase the heat to medium high and let the mixture boil without stirring. Brush the sides of the saucepan regularly with the pastry brush dipped in warm water to keep the caramel from crystallizing.

Check the temperature regularly with your candy thermometer until it reaches 250°F (121°C). (Be patient as it will take at least 20 minutes or so.) Then remove the saucepan from the heat and add the vanilla/coffee mixture, stirring thoroughly to blend. Pour the caramel into the prepared pan and let it cool for a few hours. When set, invert the caramel onto a new piece of parchment paper and cut it into squares with the sharp knife.

To make the chocolate coating, place 20 ounces of the chopped white chocolate in the bain marie (bowl over a saucepan ¼ full of water). Heat the water over medium-low heat and gently stir the chocolate as it melts. When it is completely melted, remove from the heat and gradually stir in 10 more ounces of finely chopped white chocolate, stirring until smooth. Dip the caramel squares in the warm chocolate using the instructions on pages 22–25. Place the dipped caramels on a parchment-lined pan and, if desired, sprinkle cinnamon on the top for decoration (make sure to add the cinnamon before the chocolate coating dries).

Once cut, caramels should be stored in the resealable container in the refrigerator in order for them to keep their shape. Stored properly, caramels will keep for a month.

Cinnamon is an ancient spice that was used by the Egyptians for medicinal purposes as well as for flavoring food and drinks.

Irish Coffee Caramels

Invented at Shannon Airport in the 1940s for a group of American tourists who had had a rough flight, the traditional Irish coffee consists of coffee, whiskey, brown sugar, and cream. We think the little gems here do a pretty good job of approximating that warm, rich flavor.

Makes about 72 caramels.

YOU WILL NEED

Small bowl
5-quart saucepan with tall sides
Pastry brush and a small mug of
   warm water
Wooden spoon
Calibrated candy thermometer

9 X 9-inch pan, oiled and lined
   with parchment paper
Sharp knife
Bain marie
Fork or dipping tools
Resealable container for storage

INGREDIENTS

1 teaspoon freshly grated nutmeg
2 tablespoons instant coffee or
   espresso powder
5 tablespoons whiskey, divided
2 cups sugar
1 cup light brown sugar,
   firmly packed
1 cup honey

1 cup evaporated milk
2 cups heavy cream
1/2 cup unsalted butter, cut into pieces
Pinch of salt

30 ounces white chocolate, finely
   chopped and divided
Candied rose pieces for decoration
   (optional)

Instructions:

In the small bowl, mix the nutmeg, instant coffee or espresso powder, and
2 tablespoons of whiskey and set aside.

In the saucepan, mix together the sugars, honey, evaporated milk, heavy
cream, butter, salt, and remaining 3 tablespoons of whiskey. Place the
saucepan on the stove over medium heat and stir with the wooden spoon
until all the sugar is dissolved, the butter is melted, and the mixture is
smooth. Increase the heat to medium high and let the mixture boil without
stirring. Brush the sides of the saucepan regularly with the pastry brush
dipped in warm water to keep the caramel from crystallizing.

Check the temperature regularly with your candy thermometer until it
reaches 250°F (121°C). (Be patient as it will take at least 20 minutes or
so.) Then remove the saucepan from the heat and add the nutmeg/coffee/
whiskey mixture, stirring thoroughly to blend. Pour the caramel into the
prepared pan and let it cool for a few hours. When set, invert the caramel

(recipe continues on next page)

onto a new piece of parchment paper and cut it into squares with the sharp knife.

To make the chocolate coating, place 20 ounces of the chopped white chocolate in the bain marie (bowl over a saucepan ¼ full of water). Heat the water over medium-low heat and gently stir the chocolate as it melts. When it is completely melted, remove from the heat and gradually stir in 10 more ounces of finely chopped white chocolate, stirring until smooth. Dip the caramel squares in the warm chocolate using the instructions on pages 22–25. Place the dipped caramels on a parchment-lined pan and, if desired, carefully place a candied rose piece on the top for decoration (make sure to add the rose piece before the chocolate coating dries).

Once cut, caramels should be stored in the resealable container in the refrigerator in order for them to keep their shape. Stored properly, caramels will keep for a month.

Make sure to use freshly grated nutmeg in this recipe. It has a much more intense flavor than the powdered version.

Shown here are the elements of a traditional Irish coffee: coffee, whipped cream, and whiskey.

Toffee, Brittle, Sauces, and Bars

English Toffee

If you've never had English toffee before, it's only fair to warn you: these are addictive — seriously. This buttery, crunchy confection literally melts in your mouth. And it's so easy to just keep breaking off another small piece. Before you know it, you've eaten the whole pan.

Makes about 2 pounds.

YOU WILL NEED

10 X 15-inch rimmed baking sheet
Bain marie
5-quart saucepan with tall sides
Pastry brush and a small mug of
  warm water

Wooden spoon
Calibrated candy thermometer
Resealable container for storage

INGREDIENTS

12 ounces milk chocolate and
  6 ounces bittersweet chocolate,
  finely chopped
1 cup unsalted butter, cut into pieces
1 1/2 cups sugar
1/4 teaspoon salt

2 1/2 tablespoons light corn syrup
2 1/2 tablespoons water
1 cup almonds, toasted and lightly
  chopped
1 cup almonds, toasted and finely
  chopped (for topping)

Instructions:

Butter the baking sheet and set aside.

Mix the two chocolates together and place in the bain marie (bowl over a saucepan 1/4 full of water). Heat the water over medium-low heat and gently stir the chocolate as it melts. When it is completely melted, remove from the heat and set aside to cool.

In the saucepan, mix together the butter, sugar, salt, corn syrup, and water. Place the saucepan on the stove over medium heat and stir with the wooden spoon until all the sugar is dissolved, the butter is melted, and the mixture is smooth. Increase the heat to medium high and let the mixture boil, stirring occasionally. Brush the sides of the saucepan regularly with the pastry brush dipped in warm water to keep the sugar from crystallizing.

Check the temperature regularly with your candy thermometer until it reaches 300°F (149°C). (Be patient as it will take at least 20 minutes or so.) Then remove the saucepan from the heat and add the cup of slightly chopped almonds, stirring thoroughly to blend. Pour the toffee onto the prepared baking sheet and carefully spread the melted chocolate on top. Sprinkle the finely chopped almonds over the top. Place the sheet in the refrigerator until the toffee sets, about an hour. Then break it into pieces.

Toffee can be stored in the resealable container at room temperature. Stored properly, toffee will keep for up to a week.

Peanut Brittle

This classic old-fashioned candy makes a wonderful holiday gift. The addition of baking soda gives the golden brittle its airy and crunchy texture.

Makes about 2 pounds.

YOU WILL NEED

10 X 15-inch rimmed baking sheet
5-quart saucepan with tall sides
Pastry brush and a small mug of
    warm water

Wooden spoon
Calibrated candy thermometer
Resealable storage container

INGREDIENTS

1½ cups sugar
¾ cup light corn syrup
¼ teaspoon salt
1 cup water
2 cups peanuts

3 tablespoons unsalted butter,
    softened
1½ teaspoons baking soda
1 teaspoon vanilla extract

Instructions:

Butter the baking sheet and set aside.

In the saucepan, mix together the sugar, corn syrup, salt, and water. Place the saucepan on the stove over medium heat and stir with the wooden spoon until all the sugar is dissolved and the mixture is smooth. Increase the heat to high and let the mixture bubble up, without stirring. Brush the sides of the saucepan regularly with the pastry brush dipped in warm water to keep the sugar from crystallizing. Check the temperature regularly with your candy thermometer.

When the candy thermometer reads 260°F (127°C), reduce the heat to low and mix in the peanuts and butter. Stirring constantly, continue cooking until the thermometer registers 300°F (149°C). When it reaches this temperature, add the baking soda and vanilla and mix well.

Pour the brittle onto the prepared baking sheet and let it cool at room temperature. When it is set, break it into pieces.

Brittle can be stored in the resealable container at room temperature. Stored properly, brittle will keep for up to a week.

Vanilla Caramel Sauce

This is an easy recipe that doesn't take much time, though it does require your undivided attention. With a little patience, you will be rewarded with a velvety smooth caramel sauce that is heavenly drizzled over a bowl of vanilla ice cream.

Makes about 2½ cups.

YOU WILL NEED

5-quart saucepan with tall sides
Pastry brush and a small mug of
  warm water

Wooden spoon
Medium bowl
Resealable container for storage

INGREDIENTS

1 1/2 cups sugar
1/2 cup light corn syrup
1/2 cup water

1 cup heavy cream
4 tablespoons unsalted butter
1 tablespoon vanilla extract

Instructions:

In the saucepan, mix together the sugar, corn syrup, and water. Place the saucepan on the stove over medium heat and stir with the wooden spoon until all the sugar is dissolved and the mixture is smooth. Increase the heat to medium high and let the mixture boil without stirring. Brush the sides of the saucepan regularly with the pastry brush dipped in warm water to keep the caramel from crystallizing. Swirl the caramel around occasionally to make sure it is cooking evenly.

When the caramel turns light brown, remove the saucepan from the heat and add the cream, butter, and vanilla. Stir carefully. Place the saucepan back on the stove over low heat and stir until the mixture is smooth.

Pour the caramel sauce into the medium bowl and let it set. Serve warm or at room temperature.

Store the caramel sauce in the resealable container in the refrigerator. It should keep for 5 days.

For a devilishly delicious chocolate version, stir in 1 1/2 ounces of finely chopped bittersweet chocolate right after you add the vanilla.

Coffee Cognac Caramel Sauce

This boozy caramel sauce highlighted by cinnamon and nutmeg accents is a real crowd pleaser. Serve this delightful concoction with your favorite cake, custard, or ice cream.

Makes about 2½ cups.

YOU WILL NEED

Small bowl
5-quart saucepan with tall sides
Pastry brush and a small mug of
    warm water

Wooden spoon
Medium bowl
Resealable container for storage

INGREDIENTS

4 teaspoons instant coffee or
    espresso powder
4 tablespoons Cognac
1 1/2 cups sugar
1/2 cup light corn syrup
1/2 cup water

1 cup heavy cream
3 tablespoons unsalted butter
1 tablespoon vanilla extract
1 teaspoon cinnamon
1 teaspoon freshly grated nutmeg

Instructions:

In the small bowl, mix together the instant coffee or espresso powder and the Cognac. Set aside.

In the saucepan, mix together the sugar, corn syrup, and water. Place the saucepan on the stove over medium heat and stir with the wooden spoon until all the sugar is dissolved and the mixture is smooth. Increase the heat to medium high and let the mixture boil without stirring. Brush the sides of the saucepan regularly with the pastry brush dipped in warm water to keep the caramel from crystallizing. Swirl the caramel around occasionally to make sure it is cooking evenly.

When the caramel turns light brown, remove the saucepan from the heat and add the cream, butter, and vanilla. Stir carefully. Place the saucepan back on the stove over low heat and stir until the mixture is smooth. Add the coffee/Cognac mixture and stir well. Add the cinnamon and nutmeg and mix well.

Pour the caramel sauce into the medium bowl and let it set. Serve warm or at room temperature.

Store the caramel sauce in the resealable container in the refrigerator. It should keep for 5 days.

Orange Thyme Caramel Sauce

More often found in savory dishes, thyme adds a delicate aromatic note to this delectable caramel sauce, which is further enhanced by the addition of refreshing orange zest.

Makes about 2½ cups.

YOU WILL NEED

Zester
Small saucepan
Mesh sieve
Small bowl
Wooden spoon

5-quart saucepan with tall sides
Pastry brush and a small mug of
     warm water
Medium bowl
Resealable container for storage

INGREDIENTS

1 cup heavy cream
1/4 cup fresh thyme leaves, stripped
     from stem and roughly chopped
1 tablespoon freshly grated
     orange zest

1 1/2 cups sugar
1/2 cup light corn syrup
1/2 cup water
4 tablespoons unsalted butter
1 tablespoon vanilla extract

Instructions:

In the small saucepan, bring the cream to a simmer. Remove from heat and add the thyme and zest. Set aside for 30 minutes. Strain the cream into the small bowl, pressing the solids to get as much flavor as possible. Set aside.

In the 5-quart saucepan, mix together the sugar, corn syrup, and water. Place the saucepan on the stove over medium heat and stir with the wooden spoon until all the sugar is dissolved and the mixture is smooth. Increase the heat to medium high and let the mixture boil without stirring. Brush the sides of the saucepan regularly with the pastry brush dipped in warm water to keep the caramel from crystallizing. Swirl the caramel around occasionally to make sure it is cooking evenly.

When the caramel turns light brown, remove the saucepan from the heat and add the flavored cream, butter, and vanilla. Stir carefully. Place the saucepan back on the stove over low heat and stir until the mixture is smooth.

Pour the caramel sauce into the medium bowl and let it set. Serve warm or at room temperature.

Store the caramel sauce in the resealable container in the refrigerator. It should keep for 5 days.

Pumpkin Spice Caramel Sauce

The flavors of pumpkin and pumpkin pie spice — a combination of cinnamon, ginger, allspice, nutmeg, and cloves — are evocative of autumn. Drizzle some of this fragrant sauce over a slice of pumpkin pie to further intensify its flavor or serve over vanilla ice cream or cheesecake for a delicious fall treat.

Makes about 2½ cups.

YOU WILL NEED

5-quart saucepan with tall sides
Wooden spoon
Pastry brush and a small mug of
    warm water

Medium bowl
Resealable container for storage

INGREDIENTS

1 $\frac{1}{2}$ cups sugar
$\frac{1}{2}$ cup light corn syrup
$\frac{1}{2}$ cup water
1 cup heavy cream

4 tablespoons unsalted butter
2 teaspoons vanilla extract
3 teaspoons pumpkin pie spice mix
$\frac{1}{2}$ cup canned pure pumpkin

Instructions:

In the saucepan, mix together the sugar, corn syrup, and water. Place the saucepan on the stove over medium heat and stir with the wooden spoon until all the sugar is dissolved and the mixture is smooth. Increase the heat to medium high and let the mixture boil without stirring. Brush the sides of the saucepan regularly with the pastry brush dipped in warm water to keep the caramel from crystallizing. Swirl the caramel around occasionally to make sure it is cooking evenly.

When the caramel turns light brown, remove the saucepan from the heat and add the cream, butter, and vanilla. Stir carefully. Place the saucepan back on the stove over low heat and stir until the mixture is smooth. Add the pumpkin pie spice and the canned pumpkin and mix until well blended.

Pour the caramel sauce into the medium bowl and let it set. Serve warm or at room temperature.

Store the caramel sauce in the resealable container in the refrigerator. It should keep for 5 days.

Bourbon Pecan Caramel Bars

These pecan caramel bars are classics. The combination of buttery shortbread and sweet and chewy caramel pecan filling is ambrosial. Spiked with bourbon, they exude Southern charm.

Makes about 2 dozen small bars.

YOU WILL NEED

9 X 13-inch baking pan
Large bowl
Mixer
Sifter
5-quart saucepan

Wooden spoon
Parchment paper
Sharp knife
Resealable container for storage

INGREDIENTS

For the crust
1 1/4 cups unsalted butter, softened
1/2 cup dark brown sugar,
   firmly packed
1/4 cup sugar
3 cups all-purpose flour
1/2 teaspoon salt
For the filling
1/2 cup unsalted butter, cut into pieces

1/2 cup dark brown sugar,
   firmly packed
2 tablespoons sugar
1/3 cup honey
2 tablespoons heavy cream
1/4 teaspoon salt
1 teaspoon vanilla extract
1 tablespoon bourbon
2 cups pecan halves, lightly toasted

Instructions:

Preheat the oven to 375°F (190°C). Butter the baking pan and set aside.

In the large bowl, beat the butter and sugars together until light and fluffy. Sift together the flour and salt and slowly add to the bowl, mixing until the dough looks clumpy. Press the dough into the bottom of the baking pan. Prick all over with a fork and refrigerate for 20 minutes and then bake until golden brown, about 18 minutes. Let cool completely.

Reduce the oven temperature to 325°F (160°C).

In the saucepan, mix together the butter, sugars, honey, cream, and salt. Place the saucepan on the stove over medium-high heat and stir with the wooden spoon until all the sugar is dissolved and the mixture is smooth. Increase the heat to high and let the mixture come to a boil, stirring constantly. As soon as it comes to a boil, continue stirring for 1 minute. Remove from heat and stir in the vanilla, bourbon, and pecans. Pour the filling over the cooled crust and bake until the filling begins to bubble, about 15 to 20 minutes.

Let the bars cool at room temperature. Run the knife around the sides of the pan and invert the bars onto parchment paper and then invert again onto a cutting board. Cut into bite-sized bars.

The bars can be stored in the resealable container at room temperature. Stored properly, bars will keep for up to a week.

Orange Caramel Shortbread Bars

Perfumed with the citrus notes of Cointreau and candied orange peel, these bars are irresistible. The combination of soft chewy, caramel and buttery shortbread is sublime.

Makes about 2 dozen small bars.

YOU WILL NEED

9 X 13-inch baking pan
Food processor
5-quart saucepan with tall sides
Pastry brush and a small mug of
   warm water

Wooden spoon
Calibrated candy thermometer
Sharp knife
Resealable container for storage

INGREDIENTS

For the crust
1 cup all-purpose flour
5 tablespoons sugar
Pinch of salt
1/2 cup unsalted butter, cold
   and cut into small pieces

For the orange caramel
1 cup sugar
1/2 cup light brown sugar,
   firmly packed

1/2 cup honey
1/2 cup evaporated milk
1 cup heavy cream
1/4 cup unsalted butter, cut into pieces
Pinch of salt
2 tablespoons Cointreau
2 teaspoons vanilla extract
1 1/3 cups candied orange peel,
   chopped
Bittersweet chocolate for drizzling

Instructions:

Preheat the oven to 350°F (180°C). Butter the baking pan and set aside.

In the food processor, mix the flour, sugar, and salt. Add the cold butter pieces and pulse until it resembles coarse meal. Press the crumbs into a thin layer in the bottom of the baking pan. Place the pan in the freezer for 5 minutes to firm, and then bake for about 15 minutes or until the crust is golden brown. Set aside.

Raise the oven temperature to 400°F (200°C).

Mix together the sugars, honey, evaporated milk, heavy cream, butter, and salt in a large saucepan. Place the saucepan on the stove over medium heat and stir with the wooden spoon until all the sugar is dissolved, the butter is melted, and the mixture is smooth. Increase the heat to medium high and let the mixture boil without stirring. Brush the sides of the saucepan often with the pastry brush dipped in warm water to keep the caramel from crystallizing.

Check the temperature regularly with your candy thermometer. Be patient as it will take at least 20 minutes or so to reach 250°F (121°C). Then remove the saucepan from the heat and add the Cointreau and vanilla, stirring thoroughly to blend. Add the candied orange peel and mix carefully. Pour the filling over the crust and bake for 10 minutes.

Let the bars cool at room temperature. Drizzle dark chocolate on top of the bars (see pages 25–26). When it is dry, cut into small squares or rectangles.

The bars can be stored in the resealable container at room temperature. Stored properly, bars will keep for up to a week.

Coconut Chocolate Caramel Bars

Coconut and oats add loads of texture to these chewy chocolate caramel bars. They taste a bit like those famous coconut cookes sold by girls in green uniforms. As with those cookies, one is never enough.
Makes about 2 dozen bars.

YOU WILL NEED

9 X 13-inch baking pan
Food processor
5-quart saucepan with tall sides
Pastry brush and a small mug of
   warm water

Wooden spoon
Calibrated candy thermometer
Sharp knife
Parchment paper
Resealable container for storage

INGREDIENTS

For the crust

1 cup all-purpose flour
1 cup light brown sugar,
   firmly packed
Pinch of salt
3/4 cup unsalted butter,
   cold and cut into pieces
1 1/2 cups shredded coconut
1 cup rolled oats

For the chocolate caramel

1 cup sugar
1/2 cup light brown sugar,
   firmly packed
1/2 cup honey
1/2 cup evaporated milk
1 cup heavy cream
1/4 cup unsalted butter, cut into pieces
Pinch of salt
2 ounces unsweetened chocolate,
   finely chopped
2 tablespoons coconut extract

Instructions:

Preheat the oven to 350°F (180°C). Butter the baking pan.

In the food processor, mix the flour, sugar, and salt. Add the cold butter pieces and pulse until it starts to form a dough. Transfer to a bowl and gently knead in the coconut and oats. Reserve 1 cup of dough and press the rest into an even layer on the bottom of the baking pan. Set aside.

Mix together the sugars, honey, evaporated milk, heavy cream, butter, and salt in the saucepan. Place the saucepan on the stove over medium heat and stir with the wooden spoon until all the sugar is dissolved, the butter is melted, and the mixture is smooth. Increase the heat to medium high and let the mixture boil without stirring. Brush the sides of the saucepan regularly with the pastry brush dipped in warm water to keep the caramel from crystallizing.

Check the temperature regularly with your candy thermometer until it reaches 225°F (107°C). (Be patient as it will take at least 20 minutes or so.) Then add the chopped unsweetened chocolate. Stir gently a few times and then carefully brush the sides of the saucepan. When the candy thermometer reaches 248°F (120°C), remove the saucepan from the heat and add the coconut extract, stirring thoroughly to blend.

(recipe continues on next page)

Coconut Chocolate Caramel Bars (continued)

Pour the caramel on top of the crust in the prepared pan. Sprinkle the reserved cup of oatmeal dough on top of the caramel. Bake for 20 minutes.

Remove the pan from the oven and let it cool on a rack for at least one hour. When cool, run the knife around the sides of the pan and invert the bars onto parchment paper and then invert again onto a cutting board. Cut into small squares or rectangles.

The bars can be stored in the resealable container at room temperature. Stored properly, bars will keep for up to a week.

The health benefits of oats are widely known, but coconut is also a nutritious food, rich in minerals, vitamins, and fiber.

Oatmeal Apricot Caramel Bars

Featuring oatmeal, dried apricots, and pumpkin seeds, these are one of the healthiest caramel bar treats. You will surely never find a more tempting trail mix.

Makes about 2 dozen bars.

(recipe continues on next page)

Oatmeal Apricot Caramel Bars *(continued)*

YOU WILL NEED

9 X 13-inch baking pan
Food processor
Mixing bowl
5-quart saucepan with tall sides
Pastry brush and a small mug of
  warm water

Wooden spoon
Calibrated candy thermometer
Sharp knife
Resealable container for storage

INGREDIENTS

For the rolled oats crumb

1 ¾ cups all-purpose flour
1 cup light brown sugar,
  firmly packed
1 teaspoon baking soda
Pinch of salt
1 teaspoon cinnamon
½ teaspoon ground cardamom
1 cup unsalted butter,
  cold and cut into pieces
2 cups rolled oats

For the filling

2 cups dried apricots,
  finely chopped
1 cup pumpkin seeds
⅔ cup white chocolate chips

For the caramel

1 cup sugar
½ cup light brown sugar,
  firmly packed
½ cup honey
½ cup evaporated milk
1 cup heavy cream
¼ cup unsalted butter, cut into pieces
Pinch of salt
1 tablespoon vanilla extract

Instructions:

Preheat the oven to 350°F (180°C). Butter the baking pan.

In the food processor, blend together the first six ingredients of the crumb. Add the cold butter pieces and pulse until it becomes a coarse meal. Transfer to the bowl and add the rolled oats, rubbing the mixture together between your fingers. Add two-thirds of the crumb to the baking pan and spread it evenly, pressing it against the bottom of the pan. Set aside.

Mix together the sugars, honey, evaporated milk, heavy cream, butter, and salt in the saucepan. Place the saucepan on the stove over medium heat and stir with the wooden spoon until all the sugar is dissolved, the butter is melted, and the mixture is smooth. Increase the heat to medium high and let the mixture boil without stirring. Brush the sides of the saucepan regularly with the pastry brush dipped in warm water to keep the caramel from crystallizing.

Check the temperature regularly with your candy thermometer until it reaches 250°F (121°C). (Be patient as it will take at least 20 minutes or so.) Then remove the saucepan from the heat and add the vanilla, stirring thoroughly to blend.

Pour the caramel on top of the crumb in the baking pan. Sprinkle the apricots and pumpkin seeds evenly on top of the caramel. Add the chocolate chips to the bowl with the remaining third of crumb, mix together, and sprinkle that mixture evenly over the apricots and pumpkin seeds. Bake until lightly browned, about 30 minutes.

Remove the pan from the oven and let it cool on a rack for a few hours. When cool, cut into bite-sized bars.

The bars can be stored in the resealable container at room temperature. Stored properly, bars will keep for up to a week.

Oats contain a fiber called beta-glucan, which has been found to lower cholesterol.

Creative Packaging

Who doesn't appreciate a box of homemade caramels? It's something to be treasured. One bite of the soft chewy candy can summon an array of warm happy childhood memories. And fun and inspired packaging only adds to the yummy gift's allure.

It doesn't take much to transform a plain box or a recycled one into something truly special. Following are some ideas to fire your imagination and get you started.

Small Packages for Party and Wedding Favors

Good things come in small packages, and little boxes covered in pretty flowered ribbons make lovely containers for a pair of chocolate-covered caramels.

An organza gift bag accented with a decorative rose is another great way to package a small assortment of caramels.

Store-Bought Decorated Boxes

Decorated boxes are widely available and are an easy way to impressively package your caramels.

The boxes come in many shapes and sizes.

Recycled Boxes

You can find inspiration in packaging originally used for other purposes. Add a pretty ribbon or greens and you instantly give it new life.

Decorated Candy Boxes

The addition of ribbon, papers, flowers, and buttons really jazzes up these simple white boxes.

Double-Duty Gifts

When the caramels are gone, the recipient can plant something in this lovely flowerpot.

Creative Presentation

Adding a little decorative bird and some soft moss makes this caramel-filled planter a unique gift.

Packaging Sauces

It doesn't take much to spruce up a jar — just a little raffia or ribbon will do the trick. Sometimes it's nice to attach a little clue to the flavor of the sauce, such as the cinnamon sticks shown here, or a handwritten label.

Packaging Toffee and Bars

You can package toffee or bars in little spiffed-up gift bags or a decorated take-out box.

Table of Equivalents

Some of the conversions in these lists have been slightly rounded for measuring convenienc

VOLUME:

U.S.	metric
¼ teaspoon	1.25 milliliters
½ teaspoon	2.5 milliliters
¾ teaspoon	3.75 milliliters
1 teaspoon	5 milliliters
1 tablespoon (3 teaspoons)	15 milliliters
2 tablespoons	30 milliliters
3 tablespoons	45 milliliters
1 fluid ounce (2 tablespoons)	30 milliliters
¼ cup (4 tablespoons)	60 milliliters
⅓ cup	80 milliliters
½ cup	120 milliliters
⅔ cup	160 milliliters
1 cup	240 milliliters
2 cups (1 pint)	480 milliliters
4 cups (1 quart or 32 ounces)	960 milliliters
1 gallon (4 quarts)	3.8 liters

OVEN TEMPERATURE:

Fahrenheit	Celsius
250	120
275	140
300	150
325	160
350	180
375	190
400	200
425	220
450	230
475	240
500	260

WEIGHT:

U.S.	metric
1 ounce (by weight)	28 grams
1 pound	448 grams
2.2 pounds	1 kilogram

LENGTH:

U.S.	metric
⅛ inch	3 millimeters
¼ inch	6 millimeters
½ inch	12 millimeters
1 inch	2.5 centimeters